Frontline Worshipper

Julia A. Royston

Edited by:
Claude R. Royston

BK Royston Publishing
Jeffersonville, IN

BK Royston Publishing
P. O. Box 4321
Jeffersonville, IN 47131
www.juliaroyston.com
Phone: 502-802-5385
© 2011 Julia A. Royston

All rights reserved.

No part of this book may be reproduced, stored in a retrieval system, or transmitted by means without the written permission of the author.

First published by BK Royston Publishing
Cover Design by: Julia A. Royston
Logo Designed by: Jonathan Snorten

ISBN-13: 978-0-9818135-7-8
ISBN-10: 0-9818135-7-7

Printed in the United States of America

Other Titles by Julia A. Royston

A New Season in Word: Inspirations for Divine Living © 2007

How Hot is Your Love Life? Return to Your First Love © 2008

Everyday Miracles-© 2010

Music by Julia A. Royston

Joy in His Presence – © 2004

Hymns for Him – © 2005

A New Season in Word and Song – © 2007

For Your Glory Lord—© 2009

Everyday Miracles—©2010

Published by juju 4ee Publishing

Acknowledgements

I thank my Lord and Savior Jesus Christ for giving me another opportunity to introduce more people to you. I thank you that you have entrusted this gift to me. Lord, let your Spirit move through this book to the people who will read it. Empower your people with the power to continue to fight on the frontline.

To my husband, Brian, for loving me so much that I can be and do, all that God has for me.

Thanks to all of my family for their love and support.

A special thank you to Rev. Claude R. Royston for using his fine tooth comb to edit this book.

Book Introduction

Before I begin, I must offer this disclaimer. Every church in every denomination is unique in how they worship, which songs they sing and which creative arts are displayed during the worship service. Styles of worship, music, instruments, drama and dance during worship have been heated debates for centuries. New denominations, organizations and churches have been established just because of a difference of opinion on how we are to worship God. God is so diverse in His creation that He must be just as diverse in the style of worship that He will receive. I just can't imagine that the style of worship would be as important as the heart, love and sincerity of the worship offered unto God. The intent of this book is to give foundational information, provide resources and instruction to establish, grow or revive the worship arts department in a church or ministry. The information shared should not be set in stone but, tweaked, adjusted or molded to fit your worship arts ministry at your church.

My prayer is that this book will offer you helpful suggestions. Any suggestion should be prayed over and approved prior to an attempt at implementation. One of the beauties of a book is that it can be referred to in the future. Look at your church, its worship arts ministry and the needs of the people to be ministered to, determine whether one or any of the suggestions could work in that church right now. If not, hold on to the suggestion and the need will arise and then the solution can be implemented.

Seasons and times change in the life of any organization. The church and worship arts ministries are no different. But, never say never because things change. Pastors may change, administrations change, times change and people change. My purpose is to help someone who is starting, continuing or reviving a worship arts ministry. I may never be able to consult with you one on one at your church. I pray that as you read this book you will hear my heart, feel my spirit and passion for the worship arts ministry. I have spent my life in the worship arts ministry in various capacities. I do not claim to know everything and seek to learn more and more each day. But, my hope is that I can use my experience to impart information and impact current and future generations. Be blessed as you read on...

Julia A. Royston

Table of Contents

Worship and the Frontline Worshipper	1
Do You Have the Heart for the Frontline	13
Mission Possible	25
Lead, Follow and Get Out of the Way	34
Organize, Rehearse and Rejoice	52
Singled Out	65
Retreat, Re-Charge and Re-Organize	76

Worship and the Frontline Worshipper

But the hour cometh, and now is, when the true worshippers shall worship the Father in spirit and in truth: for the Father seeketh such to worship him. John 4:23 (KJV)

Do not worship any other god, for the LORD, whose name is Jealous, is a jealous God. Exodus 34:14 (KJV)

Worship is about God.

Worship is defined as "reverent honor and homage paid to God or a sacred personage, or to any object regarded as sacred." (www.dictionary.com) True Worship is about God and not about us. There is an inherent need in man to worship or adore something. Some people worship materialistic things, other people and even themselves. True worship, however, is unto the almighty God. God is the creator of all things. He created heaven, earth and all of its inhabitants. Psalm 19:1 says the very heavens declare the glory of God. We were created for and to enjoy an intimate relationship with God. Genesis 1:1 states, "let us make man in our image and our likeness". We were created for God's glory. Isaiah 43:7 states that even every one that is called by my name: for I have created him for my glory, I have formed him; yea, I have made him. "Know ye that the LORD he is God: it is he that hath made us, and not we ourselves; we are his people, and the sheep of his pasture." Psalm 100:3 (KJV)

Worship is about God and not about us. God is truly worthy of our worship. Adam in the garden enjoyed an unobstructed and open relationship with God. But, Adam disobeyed God, broke the relationship and caused sin to come upon all of mankind. After 42 generations of time, Jesus came to bring us back into that unobstructed relationship with God again. Jesus died on a horrible cross to fulfill the plan and pay the cost of redemption by His blood and through His name came salvation. It is our privilege to receive salvation and the Holy Spirit. We should allow nothing or anyone to obstruct our relationship with God again. Our job in return is to give God the glory due unto His name through our worship. It is a privilege to worship God and because of all that He has done we should worship God even more.

Worship is directed to God.

Then the man bowed down and worshiped the LORD..
Genesis 24:26 (NIV)

The worship arts should be directed to God. Worship arts should be about God, refer to God, give glory to God, magnify God, encourage others to love and worship God more and introduce people to God. If however you minister, whether in song, dance, etc. all of your worship should be directed toward heaven, God and His attributes. The people will enjoy the performance of worship but, your worship should be unto God. You should seek to please the audience of one, God. What you do if you were standing face to face with God? Would you change anything? Would you sing that song, dance that dance, perform that poem or live that life if you really knew God was watching? Our worship is directed to God. Picture Him in your mind and whatever form of worship always remember that He is watching. It should make all of the difference in the world.

Worship is an Expression of Your Love for God.

In John 4, there is the recount of the story of Jesus and His meeting with the woman at the well. The woman at the well was famous but, she was nameless. She was a woman with a bad reputation in town. Jesus pointed out that she had had five husbands and the one she was currently with, was not her husband. Wow, this lady's reputation would make a good, award winning soap opera series storyline. I recently asked myself, why did God lead Jesus to witness to this woman of all women?

The obvious reason is that this would give her a chance to experience the love and saving grace of Jesus. But, why did God use her? The Lord said that she was selected because she was passionate and knew how to please. Well, I blushed at first but, He is correct. After the story, the scripture states "for the father seeketh such to worship Him". John 4:23 Her passion and love was used for the wrong persons and in the wrong way. God was going to change her so that her love and passion would be toward Him. Once she experienced the love of God, she would be able to direct her passion and love in the right way to the right person. Additionally, she ran into the city to tell others about Jesus so she was an evangelist and great witness to the saving power of Jesus. How much do you love God? Is He able to count on you to be His messenger? Do you love Him enough to run and tell others about how good He is to you and how He can save them too? Worship is about your love for God. Worship is about your love for God during the good and bad times. True sports fans don't love their team only when they win but, stick by their team during the bad times. That's how you know a true fan is by their loyalty and devotion during the off season and during the championship series. Well the same is true of your worship to God. Are you willing to worship Him only when He blesses you and gives you what you want?

Or are you loyal and love Him enough to worship Him when He says No to what you most desire? I wrote a devotional book titled, "How Hot is Your Love Life, Return to Your First Love? Most people think that the book is sexual in nature but, it is all about God's love for you and His pursuit of your love in return. The first of the ten commandments is that "You shall have no other gods before [a] me." Exodus 20:3 (NIV) In Exodus 34:14, God said again to have no other god before Him because He is so jealous that His name is jealous. That is clearly a jealous lover if I have ever seen one. But, God loves us with an everlasting love. God loves us with an unconditional love. When you love like God loves, it is powerful, irresistible and infectious. Who wouldn't love a God like ours? Worship then is an act that should be rooted in your love for God. Your love for God will cause you to submit to God's superiority, kingship, authority as lord and ruler of our lives. Your love to God through worship says, I am nothing without you. I can do nothing without you. I need you. You are my everything God and I don't care who knows it. As your love for God grows, your worship will intensify. It will only take a small thought to cause worship to erupt within and without you when you truly love God for who He is and not just for what He does. So what does your worship say about your love for God? Is your love hot or cold? Is your worship exciting or boring the people in the pews and God to tears? Return to your first love and watch your worship explode!

Worship is a Lifestyle.

Worship is not just an act that you do on Sunday but, your worship of God should show up in your everyday life. Worship is any act that gives glory to God. Worship can be prayer, giving, service, love, work, church, community and global outreach. Jesus said that the two commandments are to love God and to love your neighbor. The act of loving and showing love to your neighbor is another act of worship unto God. Showing love brings glory to God which in turn is an act of worship. There are acts that don't bring glory unto God. These acts are sin or short comings that must be repented from, worked through daily and forsaken. This is why worship must be offered in spirit and in truth because we need the Holy Spirit to work through us to give God the worship he deserves. What type of life are you living? Does your life give glory unto God? Does your lifestyle bring dishonor to God's name? What things do you need to change to better bring glory to His name? It is a choice that we must make each and every day to live a life that brings glory to God. Worship is the style of your whole life and not just one act or one day or one month or year. What does your life say about your worship unto God? In other words, is your life a good representation of God? Sure you are not perfect but, do you strive to live a life that would be pleasing unto God?

Worship is an Offering.

In the bible worship was filled with offerings of bulls, goats and doves that were to be sacrificed unto God for the sins of man. In the outer court there was washing, killing and burning of animals continually. Each animal was cleansed and inspected before it was offered. There was then the overwhelming smell that came from constant burning flesh. Thankfully, Jesus Christ was the final blood sacrifice needed for sin. We now worship God with our time, money, service and life unto God. What are you offering up to God with your life and your worship? Is it a sweet smelling savor or a stench in His nostrils? As much as He loves us, understands us and constantly forgives us, we must be conscious of what we are offering up to God. He is not going to accept or bless just anything. God dwells in the midst of the praises of His people. But, He doesn't have to anoint what you are offering. So, again I ask, what are you offering God in worship?

Worship Arts

In this book, the term "Worship Arts" can also be referred to as the "creative arts" or "sacred arts". I mention the word "creative arts" because some churches do use that term to mean the same as "worship arts" or "sacred arts".

For our purposes, I will use the term "worship arts" because the creative arts phrase does not always mean an expression of love or devotion unto God. The worship arts are any expression of love, glory and honor unto the true and living God. No matter how you express your worship to God, it should always be about God, for God and for His glory. The term worship arts departments will refer to the individual departments that make up the worship arts ministry as a whole. For example, you may have a dance department, drama department and praise team department which is all a part of the worship arts ministry.

Worship Arts Should be Biblically Based.

With any performance or offering of worship unto God, we should be able to refer to something in or based on scripture. Whether you open, end or have scripture in the middle of the performance, we should all conclude that it was biblically based. If there is no reference to God and/or His word then it was a performance for the theatre and not worship. In the church and worship arts, we have shied away from the term entertainment or performance because it is deemed secular. But, entertainment is defined as "something affording pleasure". Therefore, our worship arts offering should be pleasing to God and man. A performance that pleases God will be done in excellence and in sincerity. Our goal in worship should not be just to edify and encourage the people but, please the greatest audience, God.

Worship Arts Ministries Will Actively be Engaged in Spiritual Warfare.

Spiritual warfare may not be a popular subject but, it is a reality for members of any worship arts ministry. As with the natural army, you are literally on the frontline in God's spiritual army against the enemy. In Job 1:6, the scriptures states that in heaven when the angels came to report to God, that the enemy came also. If the devil came before God, what makes you think he doesn't come to your church? Therefore, when you stand in the congregation for ministry, you are not just ministering to Christians but, non-Christians and the enemy of God, himself. As a member of a worship arts ministry, the enemy wants to fight getting the message of the gospel across at any cost. Your objective is to win non-Christians to Christ. The objective of the enemy is to keep people from accepting Christ as their personal savior. Inadvertently, there will be distractions during worship and I have experienced many of those. A baby will start to cry or scream during service and have to be removed. The music CD won't play or the musician runs late. These would be distractions in worship. But, remember that greater is He that is in us than he that is in the world.

So we have the stronger, greater and supreme power on the inside of us to be victorious. In Ephesians 6:11, Paul admonishes us to put on and keep on the whole armor of God to fight against the enemy. We should stay prayerful, worship daily and feed ourselves with the word of God to be effective in spiritual warfare in worship arts ministry. If we commit ourselves to God and strive to live a life pleasing to Him, our worship will be powerful. God will be glorified, the people in your church will be edified, your pastor will be electrified and the devil will be horrified as a result of the power and presence of God in worship.

In later chapters, we will discuss the requirements of worship arts ministries members as well as give advice for an organizational structure for worship arts ministries.

Frontline Worshippers

The term "frontline worshippers" is a term that refers to not only all members of the worship arts ministry but, anybody that worships the one, the only, true and living God, Jehovah. If you are a follower of God, you are on the frontline. But, those members of worship arts ministry are truly on the frontline. "Frontline worshippers" is based in Judges 1:2 when the Israelites were faced with fighting the Canaanites after the death of Joshua.

In this scripture, the Israelites asked God which tribe shall take the lead and go first to fight and God said, "Judah shall go up." Judah in the Bible means praise. The tribe of Judah was to lead the battle against the enemy. Judah was placed on the frontline to fight against the enemy. In the end, the Israelites, with Judah on the frontline, were victorious to defeat the enemy. Therefore, worship arts ministry, your praise (Judah) must be on the frontline prepared to fight the enemy.

How do you become a frontline worshipper? A frontline worshipper is one that has repented, turned away from their old life and decided to accept Jesus Christ as Lord and Savior of their life. A frontline worshipper is sold out, committed and daily striving to live a life pleasing to God through Jesus Christ.

I have seen churches that allow people to participate and volunteer at their church without being an acknowledged Christian or member of the church. This is an individual church ministry choice and policy. I realize that volunteers and professionals are needed in non-spiritual capacities.

No matter your church policies, the ultimate goal should be to bring people to Christ and/or if they are a Christian, to a greater relationship with Christ. To be able to fight the enemy of God, you need God's power living and working in your life. You shall receive power after the Holy Spirit is come upon you. In the natural army, you always put the best soldiers on the frontline. The military special forces are sent first to infiltrate the enemy's territory and plot their attack to the defeat the enemy. As a frontline worshipper you will have inside information. You will be armed and dangerous because you've read God's word. You should be filled with His Spirit. Prayer, daily devotion and meditation should all be preparation for service and worship.

Even though you may be a Christian, you will need to be prepared and fortified to be on the frontline. Are you ready for the frontline? Do you have the heart for the frontline? Read on and we shall see.

Do You Have the Heart for the Frontline?

The heart is the key to life. You can remain alive if your heart is still beating even when other parts of your body have shut down. Your heart can keep you alive when you can't walk, talk, see, hear or move. So to the body, the heart is vital to life. In the spiritual realm, the heart is just as important. The bible states that "out of the heart, will come the issues of life." Proverbs 4:23 (NIV) What's down in your heart will come out of your mouth and then will direct your actions. Your heart will determine whether you see God because "blessed are the pure in heart for they shall see God." Matthew 5:8 (KJV) Your heart is the seat of your passions and emotions. The bible also says "For where your treasure is, there will your heart be also." Matthew 6:21 (KJV) The bible also says, "to guard your heart." Proverbs 4:23(KJV) So the heart is important naturally and spiritually. Have you ever seen people attending an event, dressed up and looking their best but, not enjoying being at the event? Your body is there but, your heart is not in it. If your heart is passionate about an activity, event, person, place or position, it shows. I agree with the saying that you should find something that you love doing so much that you would do it even if you weren't paid for it. What do you love like that? Do you love God that much?

Do you love to serve in worship arts ministry even though you may not ever get any recognition? How much is your heart in it?

Got to Have Heart

I watched the football movie, "The Replacements" with Keanu Reeves playing a quarterback for a professional team during the NFL strike. The owners still wanted to play football with older, experienced but, non-union compensated players. The coach of the team liked Keanu Reeves's character not just because he was skilled as a quarterback but, because he had a heart for the game. He had a heart to keep going during the rough times and a diligence to fight any opponent in spite of their size and skills. He had a heart for and camaraderie with each player. He understood each player's strength, weakness and how their skills could be used to win the game. In one of the pivotal scenes in the movie, one of the union professional players crossed the picket line and came back to play with the non-union players. Although he was a starter, well paid and more experienced than Keanu Reeves' character, he couldn't win because the coach said that he didn't have the "heart" for the game. For him, it was all about his car, his rings and championships but, he didn't have the heart to get hit or find a way to win. Do you have the heart for frontline worship? Are you so passionate about your service to God that you are willing to sacrifice, submit and surrender your will and agenda?

Some people are talented but, don't have the discipline to come to rehearsals or rehearse on their private time to get better. Some people are talented but, will quit when the times get tough and rough. The old saying is, "when the going gets tough, the tough get going". Some people show up for the performance and like the rewards without putting in the work.

In worship arts ministry, it is absolutely necessary that you have a heart for God, a heart for ministry, a determination and commitment to Him. Because times will be tough, difficult, disappointing and you will not always feel like worshipping. You are not going to always feel like coming to rehearsals but, that's when you have to search your heart. What's down in your heart? How much do you love God? You may enjoy the church, your friends or your particular dance, drama or singing ministry. But, there will come a time when you won't enjoy any of it. You will want to quit and may have a good reason to quit but, what does your heart say? Jeremiah said, I wanted to stop preaching, wanted to shut my mouth and quit but, it was like fire shut up in my bones. You must have the heart for it. Lord, help us to keep our heart pure toward you. Lord, help us to guard our heart against the blockage of un-forgiveness, envy, jealousy, laziness or procrastination. Lord, help us to have the heart to endure during the disappointments, difficulties and valley times of ministry.

How Hot is Your Love Life?

I wrote a devotional book entitled, "How hot is your love life, Return to your first love." This book explained thirty ways that God has been, is now and will forever love us. To continue on the frontline, you must have a hot love for God. God has to be the center of your passion and pursuit. If you pursue and place complete trust in anything else, it will fail. God's love never fails. God will always be loving, providing for and keeping us. How hot is your love life towards God? Do you have a love for God down in your heart so much that others will see and feel your love? When my husband and I were dating, people would approach us and tell us how in love we looked. They expressed that they could see that we were in love and that we had a great relationship. They didn't know what was going on behind closed doors but, could tell on the outside what was down on the inside. What does your worship say about your relationship with God? Can anyone tell that you really love God by the way you worship? Is your worship lukewarm because your heart is lukewarm towards God? Remember that "God seeketh such to worship Him" not because He doesn't have worship going on every day, all day but, because WE need to worship Him. We need to experience God's love every day through worship, His word and prayer so that we can love ourselves and then love others. It is our choice to worship God or not.

Don't feel like you are doing God a favor because you spend time with Him. He is doing you a great favor by wanting to spend time with you! He controls the universe and loves you that much to focus on you. Then it is your responsibility to love Him that much right back. Imagine that you are in a relationship with someone and you act like it is a chore every time you are with them. You give half-hearted kisses. You complain every time you have to wash clothes or dishes. You get angry if they have a need and you can supply it but, you won't. If you acted like that with me, I would say, please go on. Don't waste my time or yours by being with me. When I visit churches I notice a lot of half-hearted worship, bored looking praise and tired acting service. If you don't love God enough to do it right, sit down. God will get someone else. God will save someone else who would love to serve, love and worship Him. Remember Jesus in Luke 19:40 (KJV) said, "I tell you that, if these should hold their peace, the stones would immediately cry out". Make up in your mind, I don't want a rock crying out for me. God has shown His love to me and I must show my love back to Him. My love thermometer is on high and it is like fire shut up in my bones. So, how hot is your love life and do you have the heart for the frontline?

Out Front, Up Front and In Front

Do you have the heart for the frontline? A frontline worshipper as previously defined is a part of worship arts ministry and literally out front on the frontline in worship. When you are out front, up front and in front of people all eyes are on you. When you stand up and say "I Love God" and "I will worship Him only", everybody is watching. One of the beautiful things about a wedding is the ability for two people to stand in front of an audience of family, friends and enemies and say I love this person, I want to spend the rest of my life with this person and I don't care who knows it. A frontline worshipper should feel the same about God. I love God, I worship Him only, I am willing to stand up whether in a store front or in a stadium declaring my love for God and I don't care who is watching. This is the first quality of a frontline worshipper, "I stand for God."

Stand Up

Now, I give a person great kudos for being willing to stand up for God but, how passionate is the stand that you are taking. Can we see the passion for God that's down in your heart expressed on your face and in your actions? Therefore, my question to you is, "how hot is your love life?" I am referring to your love life toward God. Your personal love is your business but, when you are a frontline worshipper, your love life with God is seen and is everybody's business. The heart is the house of your emotions. Whatever is in your heart will eventually be known in how you speak and what you do. So the heart of a frontline worshipper should be filled with love for God. Your passion for God should be able to be seen and felt by all who watch you worship. You can always tell those who have spent time in God's presence and believe in what and who they are singing about. If you are not willing to stand up and convince the congregants of your love for God in front of people maybe you should reconsider your calling. You may not have the heart to be a frontline worshipper. When I was dating my husband and even now, people can tell how we feel about each other by the way we interact with each other when others are around us. Sure people can put on a front, pretend and masquerade about their love but, eventually, what is going on behind closed doors, will come to light. Some people say that they are not upfront people and like to worship God privately. That is great and where true worship must begin but, eventually, your private worship will demonstrate itself publicly in some shape or form. Jesus said, if you deny me before men, I will deny you before my father. The willingness to let the world know of your love for God, that is quality number two for a frontline worshipper.

Start the Fire

Next, a frontline worshipper should be able to move and ignite a fire of worship that all will feel and are willing to join. A bonfire on a fall evening is not only felt by a select few but, all who are willing to get near it. A fire is hard to be ignored. You will feel a fire's heat and be kept warm against the cold chill of the night. Fire gives light in dark places. That is the reason why forest rangers can detect a fire by the light in the night and the smoke that rises in the day. People come to church after being in a cold, cruel and dark world all week long. These same people need to be warmed by the love of God and shown the light of God's way, through His word and worship. In the entertainment industry, there is the main act and then there are warm up acts. The warm up act is to get the crowd started by telling jokes or singing music to get them ready to receive the main or featured act. A frontline worshipper should see themselves as the warm up act because each part of the worship service is important and essential for a complete worship experience. But, I must be honest, the frontline worshippers which includes all parts of the worship arts ministry, are there to start the fire. There are some people who come to church with their own fire. It doesn't matter what song is sung, who is praying or preaching, they are into the service from the beginning to the end.

I love those people and enjoy watching them worship as well as leading them in worship. But, that is not the case with every person who may be in your audience. Whether you start the fire of God's love in someone through a song you sing, an infectious smile, hand shake or hug, that should be your mission and goal for worship. I have had people come to me and say I liked your singing but, I really love your spirit. That means more to me than anything because my voice may not be sounding good one day from illness, etc. but, if you can still feel God and want a greater relationship with Him through my spirit, that's what counts the most. A frontline worshipper must be willing to give it all they have to bring the fire of God's love and the light of His great salvation to a cold and dark world.

Keep the Fire Burning

Starting a fire is wonderful but, the ability to keep the fire going is an even greater feat. I enjoy eating food from the grill. I don't enjoy burnt on the outside and raw on the inside grilled food. The key to grilled food cooked well is a great fire. Fires can be started with lighter fluid and matches but, in order to maintain a fire, you must build it on a foundation of dry wood or coals with the help of kindling. When the long burning wood catches on fire and burns for a while, the fire will be sustained to cook the meat until it's done and the flavor of the wood and smoke is deep down in it.

This flavor can be smelled and tasted when you eat the food. There is nothing better than good smoked chicken or hamburger that has the smoke flavor cooked all the way through. There is also nothing worse than biting into chicken that you wanted well done but, when you bite into it, is still raw inside and not properly cooked. Your passion and love for God is the kindling that will ignite the flame of your relationship with God. But over time and as you mature in your walk with God, you will be able to maintain this fire through the discipline of spending time in His presence, His word and His service. The long term fire of commitment, renewed worship and stable wood of His word will help move you into your purpose and destiny in your walk with Christ.

Fight the Good Fight

I considered whether the title of this book should be "Frontline Worshippers" or "Frontline Warriors" then I realized that both phrases include warfare. Both phrases denote that you are on the frontline and must be armed and ready to do battle. A true worshipper is a warrior. A Christian is a worshipper and a warrior. The enemy is seeking to kill, steal and destroy. It will take all of the spirit you have inside, the word you know and the previous experience you have gained to fight in this battle.

In the bible, Paul states that we are to fight the good fight of faith, put on the whole armor of God and when we've done all to stand. Also, the weapons of our warfare are not carnal or fleshly but, mighty through God to the bringing down of strongholds. Our power is through God and our praise is our weapon. Because we are on the frontline, we are an easy target but, must be well equipped and empowered to ward off the attacks of the enemy. Each week and at every worship opportunity you must come ready with the whole armor on and not trying to get it on. Fight on because in the end you will win.

Frontline worshippers must be strong, disciplined, mature and seek to daily develop a close relationship with the Lord. You must be able to fight the good fight of faith. Your gift, talent or ability is not enough. Worship arts ministry is not like the stage or theatre, it's not solely entertainment. You are gifted but, you must also be anointed. Having a place to display your ability or gift is not enough for worship arts ministry. Worship arts ministry is ministry. You need God and His ability, His power and His fire to do ministry effectively. Do you have the heart for the frontline? Are you willing to stand up and declare your love for God? Will worshippers be able to see and feel your love for God?

Are you willing to use every aspect of your personality and talents to bring the fire of God's love and light to a hurting world? Are you willing to discipline yourself to maintain and sustain the fire? These elements and more are essential to the heart and character of a frontline worshipper. Do you have the heart for the frontline?

Mission Possible

Where there is no vision, the people perish
Proverbs 29:18 (KJV)

And the LORD answered me, and said, Write the vision, and make it plain upon tables, that he may run that readeth it.
Habakkuk 2:2 (KJV)

For which of you, intending to build a tower, sitteth not down first, and counteth the cost, whether he have sufficient to finish it? Luke 14:28 (KJV)

Previously, we have defined worship, a frontline worshipper, worship arts and discussed having the heart for a frontline worshipper. Seeking God through prayer to maintain a strong relationship with God is primary Worship Arts Ministry. In addition to praying, we must plan. Besides praise, we must be strategic and productive. Besides shouting for victory, we must have a vision for the worship arts department. Thus, our logical next step is to visualize, create, design and develop an effective worship arts department. Ironically, I didn't say the largest worship arts department. Four bands, five choirs, three praise teams, five dance teams and two drama departments could be a long term goal of your worship arts ministry. If that is one of your goals, go for it.

Your first and number one goal should be to strive to be the most effective and anointed worship leader. In the next few chapters, we will discuss the planning, leadership, organizational structure, goal setting and implementation of an effective worship arts ministry. So let's begin.

PLANNING

What's in Your Hand and in Your House?

In the bible, God always used what people already had to begin the miracle, the development and/or the transformation into what He wanted them to be. God asked Moses "what's in your hand" and he said a rod. God said stretch out the rod. Elijah asked the widow woman to get all of the jars she had in her house and then borrow more. She gathered the jars and out of her obedience the miracle began. God used David's sling shot to take out a giant. God allowed Samson to take out an army with the jaw bone of a donkey. The first step is to analyze what you already have in your worship arts department. We will talk about leadership specifically in a later chapter but, with the swift changes in churches and worship arts departments, an inventory needs to be taken. No matter your position in the worship arts ministry, you should be able to tell who are the strengths and what are the weaknesses in your worship arts department.

No matter the church size or how long it's been in existence, what do you see in your house? You should not base your decisions solely on what or who you like but, be honest about what you see. First, take inventory of the members and their effectiveness. Whether they are your friends or not, what gift do they bring to the Kingdom and your worship arts ministry? Do they pay tithes and offerings? Do they participate with extra rehearsals? Do they stir up more mess than delivering God's message? Can you count on this person? Do they complain about everything? Mind you, I haven't mentioned anything about how well they sing, dance, act, etc. There are some super gifted people that I can't minister with because it is more trouble than it is worth. But, on the other hand, I can work with people who have a great attitude but, musically need to be developed. Pick your battles and analyze wisely. So who are the effective people in your worship arts department now? Who are the people who will be a greater asset once they are trained and continue to develop their musical gift or talent? As a member, what benefit do they bring to the ministry?

Next, what does your worship arts ministry do well and what needs work? Do the singers sing well but, have poor presentation? Do the dancers dance well but, need new uniforms? Do you need to incorporate more drama into the weekly worship services rather than just Easter and Christmas?

What would that look like and how would you convince the leadership of the church to provide additional opportunities? Would certain worship arts departments be better prepared if they had more rehearsals? Would the choir or praise team perform a more difficult song better and easier if each section was divided to work on their part individually? These are only suggestions and I hope that they help you look at your worship arts ministry differently.

Next, does your worship arts ministry need to develop mentors for younger or new members to the worship arts ministry? Does your worship arts leadership need mentors? Partnering seasoned members with new members may help to solidify and sustain the entire membership's commitment to the worship arts ministry with a high level of excellence.

I challenge you now to get a piece of paper and write down "worship arts ministry" at the top of the page. On the rest of the page divide it into two columns. In the left column, label it, strengths and the right column, label it, weaknesses. Begin listing the strengths and weaknesses of your worship arts ministry.

On the back of this same paper, title this side, Worship Arts Missing Elements. Begin listing the missing elements of people, equipment, new ministries and/or opportunities in your worship arts ministry?

If you are the leader of the worship arts ministry, plan a meeting with your pastor to discuss the strengths, weaknesses and missing elements.

So now what do you see? Hopefully, you see things that the worship arts ministry does well, needs to be improved and some goals to work toward. Additionally, I hope that this will begin a collaborative dialogue between the worship arts ministry and church leadership to improve rather that compete. Later we will talk about working together with church leadership.

Write the Vision

The bible clearly says "that without a vision, the people will perish." We just talked about determining the strengths, weaknesses and needs of your worship arts ministry. Next, we need a vision for the worship arts ministry to aim toward a goal, give direction and/or focus the ministry. Without a vision for the worship arts ministry, the worship arts ministry will perish and not thrive and grow as it should. Once you have determined the vision for the ministry, then the resources of people, finances and equipment can be used wisely.

Without a vision and mission, your ministry will be all over the place. Your funds will be spread too thin or not used at all because there was no direction or vision. In these economic times, every activity, event and project must have a plan, provision and purpose for existing. If it doesn't serve a purpose, meet a need, help to save a soul, minister to a saint or reach a goal, don't do it.

So Habakkuk said, "write the vision". So get another sheet of paper and write down what you think the vision is for your worship arts ministry. For example, to worship God, deliver the gospel through all creative forms of worship arts to save the lost and minister to the body of Christ in excellence by educating, equipping and empowering each worship arts member.

After you have your vision or mission statement, list what you currently do to support, serve and sustain that vision. Do you have weekly rehearsals? Do you have highly skilled leaders of each worship arts department? Do you have an exceptionally trained and anointed leader/pastor/minister of the worship arts ministry? Do your worship arts members live a lifestyle and maintain a spirit of worship towards God in and out of the church?

Does your worship arts ministry seek to draw people to Christ or focus on being a great form of entertainment during the weekly service?

Next, list what things need to be done to support, serve and sustain that vision. For example, we need a band director to better prepare our musicians. We need someone to periodically come in and provide bible study for spiritual growth of the worship arts ministry. We need to annually attend conferences, workshops and events to better prepare for worship. There is nothing like writing things down on paper to best determine what needs to be done. Once you have determined what needs to be done, formulate an action plan to get it done. Writing it down can't be the end of it. Making lists are only helpful for checking things off the list when it is done. Make a list but, get it done.

If You Build It, They Will Come

In the baseball fantasy movie, "Field of Dreams", Kevin Costner heard a voice calling him to build a baseball field on his farm. Costner's character builds the baseball field and magically, the Chicago Black Sox appear on the field and start playing baseball.

Now I am not promising wonderful singers, excellent musicians, ballet quality dancers and Broadway level actors are going to magically appear at your church. But, over time with consistent effort, courageous strategy, careful planning and communion with God for guidance, your worship arts ministry will grow. People are drawn to structure, organization and order. God is a God of order. God is a God of structure, organization and strategy. God built, organized and designed the universe and all of the inhabitants, creatures and plants of each planet. So do you really think that He is going to bless abundantly an unorganized, unstructured and ill-equipped worship arts ministry? I think not.

Before a house is built, there are designs of the house. Someone draws what the final house will look like. The builder has plans for every part, board and element that the house will need to be completed. The house is not built in a day but, day by day the contractor, builder and construction workers work on the house. The hole is dug deep enough for the house to stand on, the foundation is poured, the beams are placed, the lumber comes, the wires are in place, the walls are determined, the siding, windows and other fixtures come. The house starts coming together but, it started with a vision of what the house should look like. Then a plan was determined and finally the house was built by skilled and certified people according the vision and plan.

So it's time to sit down and pray, for guidance and direction from God. Then a multitude of planning needs to take place. First, plan alone then plan with the leadership team and finally, plan with the general worship arts membership. Map out a strategy, determine a budget and then allocate funding for the budget. Next, implement your plan, piece by piece, step by step and build the worship arts ministry. In the end, watch them come. God will send the people and provision you need when you have a plan, strategize your plan, work your plan and prepare everyone who will participate. If you build it, they will come.

Lead, Follow and Get Out of the Way

Lead me, O LORD... Psalm 5:8 (KJV)

Lee Iacocca the President and CEO of Chrysler Corporation coined the phrase "lead, follow or get out of the way" as a clarion call for action in the automotive industry. Mr. Iacocca used this quote by Thomas Payne to lead a complete turnaround in his company in the 1980s. I submit to you the same clarion call with a twist. As a leader in the worship arts ministry, you need to lead, be willing to follow God and the leadership of the house where you serve and then get out of the way of God. Remember that as the worship arts leader you are a facilitator of the plan and purpose of God and the vision of the shepherd of the church or ministry that you serve. Leadership is critical to the success or failure of any organization. The success or failure of any organization will be determined by the leader. The leader is the most critical and important position in any organization. Do you need a turnaround in your worship arts ministry? Does your worship arts ministry lack direction, vision, strategy or plans? If so, check out the leader.

History of the Position of Worship Arts Leader

There can be as many titles, roles and duties of the Director of Worship Arts as there are churches.

The title of the leader has ranged from Minister of Worship, Worship Arts Director, Pastor of Worship and/or Minister of Music, etc. The traditional title of Minister of Music was usually the choir director. The Minister of Music selected, taught and directed the music for each Sunday service and special holidays. The church musician played for the choir each Sunday. The title of Pastor of Worship or the Pastor of Worship Arts is basically the shepherd or leader of the Worship Arts Ministry. The pastor of worship arts should be musically gifted and trained. However, he/she should also be spiritually equipped and administratively sound to oversee each area of the department. In some churches, the members of the worship arts ministry go to the Pastor of Worship for spiritual guidance as well as worship concerns. Thus, the Pastor of Worship in that case should be an ordained a minister, pastor and trained to offer spiritual advice. The title of Minister of Music in the African American church has since been transferred to refer to the band director, coordinator or leader of the musicians. Don't let the titles in worship arts confuse you.

The basic needs of the worship arts leader, whatever the title, is to be spiritually mature, administratively organized, teachable in spirit, musically trained and possess a high level of integrity and accountability.

The Role of the Leader

And David consulted with the captains of thousands and hundreds, and with every leader. I Chronicles 13:1 (KJV)

In a play or movie, there are leading roles and then there are supporting roles in the production. The Director or Pastor of Worship Arts is clearly a leading role. The position is high profile and seen by all. On the other hand, the responsibilities in this role are great but, the criticism, analysis and scrutiny is even greater. The role of the Director of Worship must be that of communicator, leader, moderator, mediator, human resource director and music director all at the same time. No matter how talented, the Director of Worship must be able to get along with others and know how to motivate a team to achieve to their highest level. There are some people who cannot lead, work with others or lead a team. If you see yourself falling into the independent, all about me and lone ranger category, I suggest that you apply for the supportive cast role. Trying to be a leader when you should be a supporter in an organization may cause more confusion and get very little accomplished. Know the place that God has called you, get in it and stay in it.

Ministry Needs Have Changed

In recent years, churches have changed drastically. Some churches have grown exponentially and some churches have decreased in size significantly. Thus, the responsibilities of the pastor and other administrative positions in the church have changed and therefore, worship arts ministry has changed along with the church changes. First, with the fast growth of some churches, worship arts ministry has expanded beyond a single choir to include several different choirs, a praise team, praise dancers, steppers, spoken word, mime, puppets, several bands and an orchestra. People want variety and options in worship. The variety has presented an opportunity for those who do not sing or dance, to participant in the worship arts ministry. Children or youth do not have to wait until they are adults to participate in a worship service.

Who will coordinate, oversee and maintain the consistency of all of these areas, the pastor? I think not. The pastor used to do it all in a small, store-front church with one praise team and twenty members. But, even with one praise team in a store front church, a church should start organizing itself like it is a church of 10,000.

A good foundation must be established so that the worship arts ministry will grow properly rooted in a good foundation. We will talk later about establishing and organizing a worship arts department. The need to properly develop and oversee all the facets of a worship arts department should be the job #1 for the Pastor or Director of Worship. The growth or decline of worship arts departments makes the Director of Worship even more critical and vital. Placing the right leader in the right ministry helps to avoid internal organization and structural issues. As a side note, some Directors of Worship are not only responsible for the Worship Arts Department, i.e. drama, dance, music, band, etc. but, all departments or ministries that are active during the Worship service. In some ministries, the Director of Worship can be responsible for the ushers, greeters, security, music, altar workers or decision counselors and media department. This level of responsibility is tremendous and requires the person to have a great support staff, be well organized, understand the mission and vision of the church and then communicate the vision for all of the supporting areas for enjoyable worship. As a conclusion of this section, think about this. Have you seen your own congregation and ministry needs change? Do you think that the worship arts departments have changed to meet these needs? As a result, what changes have you seen in your worship arts departments, congregation and growth of the ministry, good or bad?

WANTED: Good Leaders

As much as good leadership is needed, good worship leaders are hard to find. Anointed, qualified, gifted, organized and honorable people who are committed to the worship arts ministry are hard to find whether you pay them or not. Quality leadership is not being produced in a factory, ordered easily by phone or requested by email and delivered to your door. Quality leadership still must be made, molded and refined over time by experience, submission, training, practice and performance.

What are some qualities of a good leader? What would you be looking for in a leader or director of worship? Being a good leader is complicated, multi-dimensional and there is not a cookie cutter formula guaranteed to work with every personality.

We will focus our list of characteristics on the Director of Worship, Worship Pastor or Worship Leader for the entire Worship Arts Ministry. These characteristics can be adjusted for the individual worship arts department leaders. This list will not be exhaustive but, will seek to highlight the most important characteristics.

First, a worship arts ministry leader needs to be spiritual. A leader who is spiritual is a key ingredient to leading a worship arts ministry. Remember worship arts ministry is about God and the worship of God. "God is a Spirit: and they that worship him must worship him in spirit and in truth." John 4:24 KJV. How can you be effective as a worship arts leader without knowing God? Worship leaders need to have an active, daily, consistent, disciplined walk with God. This involves reading, studying, knowing and living His word regularly. They should attend a large group, small group or individual bible study. No amount of money will produce or replace passion, anointing and a commitment to God.

Second, the worship leader needs to be mature, experienced, organized and a team player who can work with others without manipulation, abuse or deceit. I know you thought I was going to mention musically skilled next. Being musically skilled is a given but, people often overlook the importance of spirituality and character.

Next, the worship leader/director needs to be able to work well with other worship arts members as well as collaborate with those outside of the worship arts department. To be a good worship arts leader, you need to be part politician, part humanitarian, part mediator, part pastor, part counselor and part dictator. Now you may think: are you serious?

In my years of experience, I have seen the need to wear all of these hats and assume these roles. The key is being able to know when to step into which role and when. That is what experience and wisdom will teach you in the position of worship arts leader. Some people assume the role of dictator all of the time when sometimes being a politician or mediator might be best and vice versa. The ability to get along and still fulfill your mission and vision is the main reason for making adjustments and taking a slightly different position on certain issues.

Next, a worship arts leader needs to be musically skilled. The needs of the church and its congregation will determine what level of musical skill that must be. One church may need the worship leader to have a Doctorate in Music or another church may just need someone experienced who can read music, teach parts, etc. without having a degree in music. Other churches may find their needs somewhere in between. I played an instrument in high school and college but, never learned to play the piano or keyboard. I can read music and taught all of the parts for each choir I directed just from listening to each song. I sing and write songs as well. So, you can be an active and effective worship arts leader without playing an instrument. A worship arts leader who does not play must be able to work with and give clear instructions to musicians. I have great respect for and rapport with musicians. Mutual respect is an art form and must be cultivated from the start of any musical relationship.

Next, a good leader should recognize and acknowledge his/her strengths, weaknesses, resources and inadequacies. A good leader will strive to improve their weaknesses and inadequacies. On the other hand, a good leader will strive to impart their strengths and resources to others for their growth and development. A good leader is also not afraid to surround himself with people who have the abilities that he lacks. A good leader should not be intimidated or jealous of the gifts of others but, will encourage the development of these gifts and allow them to flourish and grow. In fact a good leader allows others to shine for the good of the entire organization. If this is a flaw in the leader, much prayer must be made for the leader. Over the years, I have seen many organizations as well as worship arts departments destroyed by unchecked pride and ego. If the leader has the entire worship arts department at heart, there may be times that decisions will be made to the dislike of the leader but, it is for the good and betterment of the whole organization.

Next, a good leader should be fearless when facing adversity but, be willing to humble themselves, admit to mistakes and correct them. A good leader is not one who only gives out orders for a job or task to be done but, will be the first to arrive, on the front line and in the trenches to help get the job done.

Next, the leader should be able to determine and evaluate processes as to what is working well or what needs to be tweaked. If the leader doesn't have these natural evaluating skills, they should seek guidance from trusted consultants and outsiders. These consultants should be able to give advice and clear direction to better serve the worship arts ministry. Additionally, a leader should take suggestions, criticism and feedback from the membership in an orderly fashion. Each of the recommendations should be taken into consideration and then a decision reached. Be ready to give an answer or explanation no matter how difficult when a final decision is reached.

Finally, a good leader has to be able to submit to an analysis and evaluation of their leadership ability. There will always be areas for improvement. No one is perfect. To improve and get better as a leader, you have to be evaluated. Every secular job evaluates each employee at least once a year and new employees more often. The same should be true in the church community. You should submit to an evaluation. As an artist, author, wife and teacher, I evaluate myself after every performance and ministry event. I also take time for overall ministry evaluation twice a year, in June and December. I also ask my husband and others to evaluate me. I seek evaluations from those that truly love me but, also love me enough to tell me the truth.

This is the team that you want to surround yourself with as a leader. My prayer, as should be yours, is that we all become better in whatever role God has called and ordained for each of us.

It is no easy task to be a good leader. You will need God's guidance, patience and power to survive and thrive during difficult times. To be a good leader it will take every resource, connection, advisor and counselor you trust to get it done. Are you one who is committed as long as things are going well but, quit when things aren't so wonderful? Are you going to stick to it and find a solution that is best for the entire organization? Are you able to be a fair leader to all and not just lean to the side of your friends and favorites? This sets apart a good leader from a poor one. Can you accept criticism period? Do you have the mindset of a team player, coach or motivator? Think long and hard about this questions and then answer truthfully, if asked, could I be the worship arts department leader?

Obtaining a New Leader

Your church or ministry has probably established the method of how the worship arts ministry director should be selected. Most churches interview and hire the minister of worship, musicians, director of the choir, etc.

Smaller churches may not have an overall Worship Arts Director but, will appoint a choir director, choir president, dance ministry choreographer, etc. for each worship area separately. In those instances, the pastor or administrator may be in charge of all parts of the worship service. No matter the organizational structure or title, the leader is a very important position. Whether you are leading all of the departments or just one, lead with excellence. As the leader you will cast the vision and be held accountable for ever decision, performance and project of the worship arts ministry. You are the captain of the ship and will chart the course for subsequent growth or destruction of the worship arts ministry or your specific department. In my home church, one of the elder deacons used to sing a song that said, "let Jesus lead you all of the way."

Follow

Wherefore I beseech you, be ye followers of me. I Corinthians 4:16 (KJV)

Following Brings a Level of Trust

Growing up I was always taught that you couldn't lead, if you couldn't follow. Being a good follower, demonstrated to my parents, teachers and church leaders that one day I would be given the chance to lead.

The ability to follow, serve and learn from another leader is important, whether you agree with that leader or not. Observe, listen and internalize all that you see and hear from this leader. You don't know where God will place you in the future. The lessons learned will be a great resource and hopefully, you will not make the mistakes of your predecessors.

Following in a New Culture

I often find that people who lead corporate or secular organizations automatically feel they can lead in the church or worship arts setting. I am not negating your leadership ability but, the transfer is not always smooth from the corporate arena to the church setting. Leading in the church setting is a different culture unto itself. The culture, customs and people are different in the church setting. The secular setting relies on your work experience and educational know how for promotion and leadership qualities. The church should not only look for these same qualities but, your spiritual maturity and insight. Some actions, projects or programs may be good, right and appropriate but, implementation needs to be accurate, timely and with the spiritual unction and motivation. Following in the new church environment for a period of time will give you information, insight and instructions and then produce a better spiritual leader rather than an educated leader.

As the worship arts leader, you will be accountable to God, the pastor and the leadership of the church. As the worship arts leader, you will be criticized by the members at large. As the worship arts leader, you will not like what the pastor, church leaders or members have to say at times, but, in the new culture you can't do, say or act any kind of way. Although some do, a good leader/follower, spiritual leader/follower and Godly leader/follower cannot do, say or act any kind of way if they want to be pleasing to God. Sometimes you will have to bite your tongue, hold your thought, count to 100, pray hard and then smile.

Following Gives You an Inside View

Have you ever noticed that some people that are the most critical of a program, job, organization or group have never volunteered, worked or participated in that organization? As a teacher, I have a principal and see how hard they work. I know some of the hard decisions, choices and at times, unreasonable mandates sent down from higher authorities. Because I follow and have worked closely with the leader, I have no real desire to be in that position. I have had an up close, ring side seat into that leader's role and it is not pretty. It makes me think about what type of leader I would be in that situation.

Finally it makes me not so critical of the person or position. Following and working closely with a leader will give you an inside view of what the problems, decisions and resources are so that the organization can be its best.

Everybody Must Follow Somebody

The ultimate person that you must be willing to follow is Jesus Christ, His word and His way. Paul said, "follow me as I follow Christ." Are you following Christ? As a worship arts leader, you should seek to live a life of obedience to the word of God. It is a good idea to preface your actions and words by asking, what would Jesus do?

Whether you are in a paid or voluntary position, you are accountable to the pastor and leaders of your church or ministry. As stated before, whether you agree or not, you must strive to follow the rules and procedures of that ministry. Otherwise, resign and move on. If there is an issue of great importance to the development and growth of the worship arts ministry, make an appointment and sit down professionally and rationally to come to some resolution. Open rebellion and inappropriate confrontation with the intent to embarrass or call on the carpet a leader is not a good idea.

I have seen people do it and even if the pastor or leader was wrong, the reputation of the person who launched the attack is usually ruined in the process. There is a right way and wrong way to do anything. It would be better to part ways agreeing to disagree than to create contention within the church and among the leadership.

Remember somebody is always watching you. From the smallest child to the oldest adult, people are watching you. I sing at churches and small children who could barely talk, come up to me and can't call my name but, they recognize my face from leading worship that day. No matter how little you may consider your ability or actions, someone is looking up to you. As children, we learn how to be adults by watching our parents. You are a role model whether you want to be or not just because you are the leader. People are learning how to be leaders by watching you. People are learning how to handle difficult situations, motivate a team or be a better singer or worshipper by watching you. People are learning about your relationship with God by watching you. People get insight into your life and journey by watching you. People are following you because they also believe in you and your abilities. Are you a good follower? Ask yourself how well are you following the leader? Do you think that your following would ever allow someone to trust you to be the leader? Can you lead and thrive within the church setting and culture?

Are you following so close that you have an inside view of what it's like to lead? Are you mindful that someone is always watching you? We will all know how great you lead by how well you follow.

Get Out of the Way

And the Spirit of the LORD began to move… Judges 13:25 (KJV)

As a worship arts leader, you can plan, practice and prepare as much as humanly possible. In the end, you have to be willing to let go of your way and step aside and let God have His way. Remember it is not about you but, about God. I come from a Pentecostal/Apostolic denominational background. Church services were very spirit led and no service was ever the same as the last. We usually didn't have written programs because we didn't always follow them. There was a usual order of service but, anything could happen at any given time. The worship leader, choir director, musicians, deacons, mothers and pastor had to be ready to shift gears at any time in a service. I realize that most people couldn't handle that kind of service. At times, all of our worship planning would go flying out the window because God's plan for that service didn't agree with our plan.

I was raised in that atmosphere and can easily flow in that style of worship. There are other worship services that are the exact opposite. Each service is going to run primarily as planned. The hymnal, praise songs and sermon will be different but, it will run exactly as planned every service. There may be special musical guests, guest preachers and a special presentation but, overall, the worship is planned and timed to each detail. I have led worship in these services and can truly say that God directs, orchestrates and gives His direction during the worship planning process. I have no problem planning and worshipping in that type of atmosphere. I can clearly see the intent, meaning and direction of the worship service and have enjoyed them immensely. God is a strategic God. He doesn't do anything without thought, intent and purpose. It matters not whether God interrupts or instructs the worship, just make sure that God is involved and the object of your worship. Know that you are God's vessel to be used how He sees fit. Offer and yield your body as the sacrifice, your gift as the instrument and then get out of God's way. Let Him have His way through and in you. Be a great leader, be an even better follower but, before you get run over, get out of God's way.

Organize, Rehearse and Rejoice

> So the service of the house of the LORD was set in order
> 2 Chronicles 29:35 (KJV)

In the previous chapter, we spent an extensive amount of time talking about the worship arts leader/director/pastor position in the worship arts ministry. Once the leader is in place, the worship arts ministry must be organized.

Organization

The worship arts ministry should be organized and have a strong, skilled and seasoned administrative staff and officers. If you are a newly formed church, organizing your worship arts ministry will be fresh, new and built on a good foundation. If your worship arts ministry is established but, not well organized, get organized. It may be time to get out all of the handbooks, membership guides and directories to be revisited and revised. People have come and gone. Some policies, procedures and practices may be obsolete and no longer necessary. You may be holding people accountable for rules that were fitting in 1960s but, it is now 2011.

Where are we now, what should we be doing immediately and what should be our long-term goals?

There is no way that this book can feasibly address every scenario that exists in each church and ministry. I will attempt to give general and basic needs of every worship arts ministry no matter the size or make up.

Ministry Needs

First, determine what departments are currently needed to make up your worship arts department? What type of leadership will be needed in these departments? For example, will you need a worship arts pastor and then worship arts leaders for each department or a combination of both? Will officers be needed in each department or just one set of worship arts ministry officers that will govern each individual department? Once the current overall needs of your worship arts ministry have been decided, note how often these needs will be revisited and revised. Annually or every 2-3 years or as the need arises?

Organizational Structure

Next, the organizational structure of the worship arts ministry should be established. The need for officers, music directors, choreographers, musicians and administrators should be determined for your specific worship arts ministry.

All of the positions listed do not have to be an immediate need. Grand ideas of the future are wonderful but, focus on the present, keep all things in the proper perspective and the plans for the future will come to fruition. Job descriptions should be written. A job description should be supplied for every position whether it is a paid or voluntary position. Often there are too many people walking around doing a lot of things that are not their job. If everyone has a job, knows what their job is, is qualified for their job then, a lot can be accomplished. What are the skills, education and duties of the position? What will the person do in that position? Who will the person answer to in this position? If the person leaves the position, how will a new person be selected?

This organization structure can be complex or simple depending upon the needs of your church or ministry. The organizational structure should be written and reviewed by every staff member. Once the organization structure has been approved, the membership of the worship arts ministry should receive a copy and procedures for contacting people on the organizational structural chart should be outlined and discussed. This will give the membership a person to contact, how they are to be contacted, email, hours, etc. and what appropriate situations that person will be responsible and held accountable. If the situation is not handled, who do you contact to make sure that the situation or problem is resolved.

Handbook

Next, a handbook of procedures, policies and practices should be established and maintained for a worship arts ministry to run smoothly. A worship arts ministry may have several departments with different rehearsals, performances and policies. Members of the worship arts ministry are mainly volunteering their time and do not want to waste time. We should be good stewards of God's people's time and resources.

The member handbook should include the qualifications and expectations for membership, distinguish an inactive from an active member and what actions disqualify you from continued membership.

The Handbook Should Include:

A list of each department in the worship arts ministry, i.e. dance, mime, praise team, choir, etc.

A mission statement, vision statement and purpose for each department of the worship arts ministry

History of each Department in the worship arts ministry

Moral Code of Conduct

Rehearsal schedule

Performance schedule

Uniform (be specific about the uniform because some people can't be left to their own judgment.)

Dues or Assessments

Membership directory form

Special events that the group will perform

Contact information for the officers of each worship arts ministry

Member Directory

Next, there should be a directory of all of the worship arts ministry members. This directory should include all contact information, birthday, anniversary, interest, skills, application date or date the member joined the worship arts ministry. The members should know how they will receive notices or updates whether through email, text messages, twitter or postal mail. Annually or semi-annually this directory should be revised and updated with new members, inactive members or changes in contact information. The secretary or administrative person should be responsible for maintaining the member directory.

Music Documentation

If sheet music or lyric sheets are provided for music, then a folder or binder should be required for each member. These folders or binders can be supplied by the ministry or the member. It is always nice to provide these materials if the budget of the ministry is able to support it. If there is not budget enough, then raise the budget or each member will have to supply his own folders or binders. The music secretary should organize and keep a copy of all original music. If your worship arts department does not have a music secretary, one can be established or this can be responsibility of the general secretary. A music secretary is a vital and critical part of the music ministry staff.

Song Directory

Begin compiling a list of each song that you currently perform or have performed and the original key of the song. There should be binders that contain copies of the sheet music and/or lyric sheets for each song. Musicians, lead singers and choir members change but, this list and collection process should remain constant. An electronic version of the songs' lyrics should be created and available with copyright information for the media ministry. The copyright information should include the artist, writer, title of the song, publishing company and year of copyright.

The artist who sings the song and writer of the song are not always the same person. If you have the original CD packaging, copyright information should be available for each song. Additionally, visit one of the three U. S. Performing Rights Organizations, i.e. ASCAP, SESAC or BMI. Their websites contain databases that can be searched for the copyright information for any song registered. You can search by song title, writer or recording artist. This is a time consuming process and must be done weekly for each song.

If there is music used by the drama, dance or spoken word departments, there should be a duplicate copy of this music. I suggest that the same CD that is used in rehearsals should not be the same CD used during performance. What happens if someone gets sick and doesn't show up on Sunday? The ministry must go forth.

Order

Once your procedures, policies, practices, leaders and officers are in place and agreed upon, follow them. God is a God of order. Everything He created was in order. He expects order in His house. God blesses things that are in order. These policies should be revisited annually and changes made. On the other hand, don't attempt to bend or adjust these rules for favorite people and then insist that others follow the rules.

Be fair and judge right. If there is order in God's house then God will be bestow blessings in His House.

Rehearse and Rejoice

And when they were come, and had gathered the church together, they rehearse... Acts 14:27 (KJV)

Rehearsals are critical to the development, growth and structure of the worship arts ministry. Rehearsals are where instruction is given, new music or routines are learned and we become a team to minister to God and His people. We have discussed at length about the leadership of the worship arts ministry and how this position is critical to the worship arts ministry. The rehearsals will reflect the leader and the vision for the ministry. If the rehearsals are haphazard, unorganized and non-productive, the performances will be ineffective, poorly performed and have a reputation of inadequacy. A spirit of excellence must be emphasized and mandated. But, more importantly, excellent actions, responsibility and accountability must be required. Each worship arts ministry will have its own rules and regulations but, if you aim to be mediocre, you will receive mediocrity. If you aim for perfection, you should receive excellence. It all depends on the standard for your worship arts ministry.

Do you want your worship arts ministry to be like every other church's on the block or do you want to have a worship arts ministry that stands out from all of the rest? It's up to you.

Rehearsal Structure

I can't stress enough about the importance of a worship arts ministry being structured and organized. Each rehearsal should be structured and organized. Adjustments may have to be made because of attendance, emergencies or worship planning but, there should always be a plan and goal to be reached at each rehearsal. People's time is valuable and when you waste time, you are subject to lose people and commitment to the ministry. The worship arts ministry leaders should have a schedule of when what group or ministry will minister. If you only have one choir, you know that choir will sing every Sunday. But, if you have one adult choir, one children's choir, a women's choir and the brotherhood choir, you should determine when each of these choirs will sing, perform, etc. throughout the entire year. The rehearsals for these particular groups should be set and the calendar of these dates distributed to each worship arts ministry member. Again, I realize that adjustments may have to be made and additional rehearsals scheduled or some rehearsals cancelled but, you should at least start with a planned rehearsal schedule.

Prior to the rehearsal, the leaders, musicians, choreographers, music secretary and media ministry personnel should meet and plan together. Once the order of worship and music has been established, assess what the needs are for this service. Will additional musicians be needed for this service? What will be the logistics or staging of the service? What are the media needs, i.e. tracks, microphones, video and rent or bring in additional equipment? The purpose and/or theme of the event or service should be discussed. Will there be a special guest soloists, preacher, musician or psalmist? What will be the special guests' needs? Each individual at the pre-rehearsal should have clear assignments and adequate time. Be sure to complete these assignments prior to the rehearsal and/or event or service. I realize unexpected emergencies arise but, failing to plan means that you plan to fail.

Before Rehearsal

Prior to the rehearsal time, the music secretary should have the lyric sheets photocopied. These same lyrics with copyright information should be given to the media department for each song sung, danced to or needed for general congregational worship. The band or musicians should have practiced and be prepared to play the songs for the congregation, choir, praise team or soloists. The CD or iPod player should be ready for the dance ministry.

The drama department should have their parts duplicated and ready to distribute. The directors/leaders should be ready and prepared to teach the parts, dances and lines for each rehearsal. This is an example of a worship arts ministry that is working with the spirit of excellence.

During Rehearsal

Like any other meeting of Christians, there should be prayer specifying any needs of the members, scripture and an opening praise song. Announcements, calendar changes, new events and uniform discussions can be done right after this or at the end of rehearsal. I prefer taking care of the business of ministry at the end of rehearsal because there will be those that come in late. It will be the job of the general or corresponding secretary to send out reminders and notices to those who do not attend or leave early.

Keep the rehearsal moving and timely by limiting talking, walking and distractions of the worship arts members. Additionally, if the leaders and musicians are prepared, the planned music to be covered should be accomplished. The decorum and expectations for rehearsals should already be placed in the member handbook. I have been a part of groups that have fines and penalties for lateness, etc. I encourage you to have a warm, welcoming and organized atmosphere and people will be on time and continue to come week after week.

There are people who will be late because of work schedule, a tire blow out or just heavy traffic. Pick your battles. Do you waste time trying to collect fines and fees for excused lateness or do you work on making the ministry and delivery of the message the best? I lean toward the latter. I agree with order, structure and organization but, make sure that there is a balance between order and obsession.

Rejoice

Rejoice evermore. I Thessalonians 5:16 (KJV)

Each rehearsal should be a time of worship and fellowship as well as learning and perfecting new music, liturgical dance routines or speaking lines for a new dramatic play. Worship arts members are people who have struggles, hardships, illness, death, birthdays, anniversaries, new babies and other reasons to celebrate. There should be time allotted to share their joy, pain and/or disappointment. With a ministry of mature Christians, people should be able to find encouragement, comfort, empowerment, information and instruction on their Christian journey. During rehearsal, I have seen people find employment, repair men, buy a used cars, get a jump for their car and new tires as a result of their testimony.

We should celebrate with our members by having wedding and baby showers, rejoice for promotions and the like and all levels of educational pursuits. We are the body of Christ. When one member hurts, we all hurt. When one member cries, we all may shed a tear. When one member gets married, has a child, gets a job or is healed from a cold, we should all celebrate. There will be some people who will attempt to take advantage of the situation and if so, a gentle reminder and encouragement should be given to keep moving forward in the faith. The leaders should be discerning enough to know when to cut the rejoicing off and move forward with the rehearsal. But, remember that rejoicing is also a part of worship and again, I say, rejoice.

Secondly, worship arts members should feel that they are a part of the family of God as well as a member of the worship arts ministry. As a family, we should all want each member to live the abundant life in Christ, spiritually mature, becoming a disciple, fulfill their purpose and achieve their personal goals. Our number one goal of worship arts ministry is to worship and serve God but, our next goal is to see people brought to Christ, know Christ better and grow in Christ.

Next, worship arts members should experience the presence of God during rehearsals. There should be times that the music stops and we all lift our hands and worship.

There should be times that some may run, shout, dance or cry. In God's presence is the fullness of joy. Whether you have rehearsal on Monday or Saturday, people need a time of refreshing, refilling and refueling for that day or week. Where the spirit is, there is liberty. You may be singing, dancing or telling about the goodness, power or mercy of God. At times, you can't help but, get full, overwhelmed and emotional about how great and good our God is to us. So has God interrupted your rehearsals lately? Have you gotten out of His way to allow Him to have his way? Do members feel better when they are leaving rehearsal than when they came in? If they do, they will be back and some will come on time.

Singled Out

The LORD will single them out.. Deuteronomy 29:21 (NIV)

Singled Out

In the past 40 years, I have been a part of praise teams, the lead singer for many choirs, I've sung solos for many funerals, weddings, banquets, tent meetings, revivals and conferences. I have a heart for those that are the lead singer of a choir, sing a solo or are a part of a praise team. So that I am not repetitive with these three areas I will simply say, the singled out. The singled out position is up front. Everybody sees you when you are singled out. If you are the lead or soloist, everybody hears you when you are singled out. It is viewed as a very prominent and envied position and place to be when you are singled out. People try all types of things to position themselves to be among the singled out. As one who has been singled out for years, I will try to give you a hint of what it is really like and what is necessary to be singled out.

Singled Out Should be a Leader

The singled out is a position of leadership. Even though the singled out may or may not be the director or pastor of worship, she is a leader.

It doesn't matter whether the singled out ever hold an office, they are leaders. Do not place anyone in a singled out role unless she/he is a good leader but, an even better follower. Some people cannot handle the position of the singled out. The singled out position has turned some people into divas, prima donnas and the like. The singled out position has turned some people's attitude sour and made them believe that someone owes them the position, song or place on the praise team. The old saying goes, "new levels, new devils." The reality is that the more you are featured, singled out and selected, the more problems, attacks and criticism you will face. If you can't handle singing with others in your choir section, don't try being a part of the singled out group. You may want to be on display but, you'd better be ready to "bring it" as the young people say, when it counts.

Singled out Should be Anointed

As a singled out, frontline worshipper, you need to bring the anointing that destroys every yoke. As a singled out singer, you need to be able to connect with God and usher in His presence and not just rely on your gift and talent. As one who is singled out, you must make sure that you are prayed up as well as practiced vocally and musically. The attack of the enemy will happen anywhere at any time.

I have noticed a pattern in my own life. Every time that I have a major ministry event to attend, some distraction, opposition or problem will arise. I am usually under stress anyway but, the enemy knows this and tries to come against me. But, greater is He that is within than He that is in the world.

Singled Out Should Be Mature

The singled out must be mature. You can't be a wimp or a baby amongst the singled out group. You must be rooted and grounded in your faith, your position in God and your place in the worship arts ministry. The singled out will be the most criticized because you are just that, singled out. The singled out should not only be the best singers but, should be the best, most passionate and mature worshippers. It is easier to turn a great worshipper into a better singer than it is to turn a great singer into a worshipper. The old saying goes, if you can't take the heat... You fill in the blank of that saying.

Singled Out and Disciplined

As fore stated, I have a heart for the singled out. I know what it is like to be in this group of people. I know the discipline of being singled out. I don't get to eat the foods, drink the cold drinks or stay up late as others who are not singled.

I am very aware of staying away from caffeine, milk product foods and getting plenty of rest to be musically my best. Being singled out, you must be disciplined. I can't eat ice cream, sherbet or a lot of cheese before I sing. I keep a wrap or scarf around my neck if there is a cold draft or air conditioning even if it is 100 degrees outside. At the slightest cold, sinus infection or ailment, I attack it immediately. I am cautious whether I am to sing on the weekend or during the week. If I am tired I try to take naps prior to singing with time enough to prepare my throat again before I sing. Athletes who want to be fit and play for a long time follow the same regimen. Good athletes train, prepare their minds and bodies to be in tip top shape for the competition. The singled out should be no different than a first round draft pick athlete. Stay physically, mentally and spiritually disciplined for service.

Singled Out are Messengers

Some soloists are excellent. I have my favorite soloists. I become ecstatic when I hear them sing. Also, after I hear them, it makes me want to sing. These soloists "bring it". They not only sound good but, give their all to convey and minister the message of the song in addition to being skilled musically.

When you see and hear singers like Tramaine Hawkins, Vickie Winans, Dottie Peoples, Shirley Caesar, Beverly Crawford, Ce Ce Winans sing, they give it their all and hold nothing back. They believe in what they are singing and will give their last breath to make sure you know and get the message.

Other soloists leave you bored and wishing they had never taken the microphone. Some have sounded off key, lost the beat, couldn't find the tempo and confused the band or musician. These soloists I categorize as shower soloists. Shower soloists are only accompanied by the music, words and tempo in their heads. They don't worry about phrasing, pronouncing words or if they are on key. They are free styling. It sounds wonderful only to them. These same people may be fine in a section but, not very effective singled out.

The Singled Out Have Good Timing

There was a sister in our choir that had a wonderful voice with a personality to get a song across but, we had to work hard with her on her timing. She either came in too fast or lagged behind too slow. If she came in on time, there was nothing stopping her but, we held our breath every time she came to the microphone to sing.

We never knew if she would be off or on with her timing. The musicians, choir members and director were fully aware of her timing problem and would encourage her often but, it was taxing to say the least. You should practice as much as possible singing along with the lead of the song. On the other hand, there are sometimes when you should stop singing and just listen for the music changes and rhythm of the song.

The Singled Out are Developed

I led my first song with the Junior Choir at my church at the age of 9 years old. I will never forget it. The songs was "Weeping may endure for a night but, joy cometh in the morning". I put the microphone at my mouth, stood straight as a board with my eyes closed in one spot until the song was over. I never saw the audience or looked at the director the entire song. I knew the different parts of the song by listening to the changes from the piano and organ but, not the director.

After my first lead, my church, my parents and I realized I had a gift to sing. I can't remember whether I asked for a record player but, my father bought me one. As a matter of fact, it was a very nice record player stereo system with separate speakers in addition, to a turn table. I spent hours in our basement practicing with the record player and the repeat handle stem left out so it would repeat over and over again. If you ever had a record player, you know what I mean. My father then realized I needed a cassette tape player as well. The choir director began giving me cassette tapes to learn the new songs to lead. My mother's job was to make sure that I had the proper clothing including very restrictive undergarments to look presentable on any stage or church. My mom taught me how to sit like a lady or stand tall and not slouch. My parents were giving me the resources and instruction to be a successful soloist. My job, on the other hand, was to practice, practice and more practice. I sang along with the lead first. I learned the lead part until I could sing the verse and all of the ad lib parts verbatim. I didn't sing in front of the mirror just in the basement alone. I watched all of the soloists at my church, other churches, regional and national conferences that I attended with my parents. I watched how they moved their hands, looked at the audience and moved about the crowd. It was exciting to watch others and even in my teens I wasn't ready to copy them per se but, I was taking notes. I needed more practice. I needed to get more comfortable with my gift. I needed to be more mature in my walk with God. Once I had more experience with God, I was a better representative and messenger of His power and goodness. Sometimes you must go through something before you can speak about it.

Once you go through something you can truly be an effective witness and not just go on what someone else said or did.

If you desire to be a soloist, listen, watch and learn from other soloists. What did the soloist do right before he or she started singing? Did the musician give a short introduction and then they began to sing or did they start the song and the musician picked it up? Did they take a deep breath before singing or was the breath slight and really unnoticeable. Knowing a song backward and forward will make you more comfortable with singing before audiences and will help, not stop, becoming overly nervous.

Did the soloist talk or introduce the song? It took me many years before I could introduce a song. If I got excited or talked too long, I would start in the wrong key. Over time I had to develop the ability to introduce a song. Then, calm myself and my nerves to make sure I started in the right key and with the right words. I had to develop this skill because I was going to sing in places where the musicians didn't know the songs I would sing. After I began writing original music, I realized the true value of introducing the song. People need to be able to connect to the message of the song even if it is unfamiliar. Also, being able to connect scripture, experiences and current events with the songs that I sing will help with conveying the message of the song.

If you really want to be good at singing solos, you must learn from others but, get your own style. Practice singing in front of the mirror and look at yourself singing. Is your face appealing or are you frowning and look mean when you sing? Does your family or friends ask you to sing for family events? If you are humming a song, does anyone ever ask you to sing it rather than hum? If so, you may be on your way to being a soloist.

Are You Really Someone Who Should be Singled Out?

This is a question that you must ask yourself. Some people would say no immediately. Others might not know the answer to this question because the opportunity has not presented itself. There are others who sing lead with the choir or even with the praise team but, struggle with actually being a soloist. These people have musical skills but, their personality and persuasive skills need to be developed. Choir directors and leaders can work with you to develop into a good lead or soloist. When you listen to a choir song, if you naturally sing along with the lead part, prior to the choir coming in, then you might consider leading a song with practice.

If you are really unsure, schedule a meeting or audition with your director and a musician.

Be prepared to hear the truth and receive helpful criticism to improve your ability. If you are not ready right then, go back again. Remember being among the singled out takes time, practice and is developed over time. Even if you have been singled out for many years there is still more to learn and ways to improve. Take courage singled out soloists, praise team member or lead singer. God sees, hears and knows all about your heart and love for Him. He has not forgotten about you. Keep moving forward by doing His work for great is your reward down here and in heaven.

Retreat, Re-charge and Re-Organize

Now go; I will help you speak and will teach you what to say.

Exodus 4:12 (NIV)

In today's society, every career and industry is competitive and you must use all of your abilities, products, marketing, people and promotions to remain viable and profitable. People that have to work, work hard. People, who don't work, work hard at not having to work. We are all working hard at something. But, in the midst of the hard work, we can lose sight of the real mission, vision and goals of the organization while working hard to make a living. In the teaching field, it's really not about making money as much as it is a great attempt to transfer knowledge to produce the next generation of great thinkers, artists, scientists and decision makers of the world. To keep on top of the curriculum and teaching techniques, it is required that we complete a certain number of professional development hours each year. Doctors, lawyers, engineers, hairstylists and other industries require the same continuing education to keep their license current and skills sharp.

It is amazing that some churches don't allow or require their worship arts ministers to have the same type of continuing education training and skill development. There is no wonder that each service looks, sounds, feels and is planned the same. There are people asleep, others checking their phones and walking in and out. What's wrong? It's stale. It's old and it's boring. God is a perpetual, moving and vibrant God. He remains the same all powerful, knowing, loving, eternal God. But, God is always mixing it up. God is always keeping you guessing. God is always taking us to another level. God is always challenging our thinking, expanding our territory and giving us new and creative ideas. With those things said, we are going to discuss some things that all worship arts ministries should do to keep the ministry alive, fresh and moving.

Teaching, Workshops, Guests and the Word

Guide me in your truth and teach me... Psalm 25:5 (NIV)

The first way to keep your ministries fresh is through teaching. Determine what the teaching is designed to accomplish. What is the goal of the teaching? Some worship arts ministries need more teaching to develop musically and/or their presentations. Other ministries may have a guest that delivers a targeted bible study to develop spiritually.

There may be administrative needs within the ministry for better organization and record keeping. One repeated and continual need is to conduct team building exercises and activities to build stronger relationships and unity. Whatever the need is, locate the books, videos or people necessary to teach you how to solve that problem or meet that need.

Now you may say, "I teach the praise team, choir, dancers and drama ministry every week". Your teaching should never stop but, sometime you need to bring in a guest teacher to give a different voice to the same information. People often don't receive from the familiar. The same teaching can be delivered by a guest but, somehow sounds more profound just because it came from a person with a different face. Don't take it personal just be happy that the message is being delivered and your teaching is being confirmed.

If a church or ministry budget is not sufficient for a guest teacher, ask the teacher if he would be willing to accept a love offering. Take a collection from the worship arts ministry members and provide the teacher with an honorarium.

After the teaching has occurred, have adequate follow-up evaluations, exercises and action plans. What did we learn?

What steps are we going to take to change for the better? What will be the time line for these changes? Will it require a church board decision or can we make these changes internally? Draft a commitment statement for the changes so that real results can take place as a result of the guest teacher. There is nothing worse than sacrificing your time to learn and the teacher's time to teach but, see no results. Follow-up and follow through with what was learned will be a key to changing behaviors that lead to ineffective ministry.

Conferences

Plans fail for lack of counsel, but with many advisers they succeed. Proverbs 15:22 (NIV)

If your ministry budget can support you or you are willing to make the sacrifice, it is good to attend conferences, workshops and/or seminars out of town. Attending national conferences allows you to mix, network and communicate with a diverse group of people with experiences that will encourage, enlighten and educate you so that you can better serve in your local worship arts ministry. There is new music that is released that may never be heard on your local radio station that will expand your music repertoire.

The national conferences have musicals and/or showcases of choirs, praise teams, dancers and soloists to demonstrate new music, variations on old music, performance techniques, uniform samples, etc. There are workshop leaders that you could communicate with to possibly be a mentor, providing advice and guidance anonymously. Be careful about naming names because with the Internet the world is very small but, it is good to get outside advice in generic, hypothetical terms. There are companies that release and demonstrate products, services and software at these conferences that can provide new ideas for worship even if your budget will not allow you to purchase. Sometimes it is just good to get away from your local city, church and worship arts ministry to get a fresh vision. Getting away can help you to return with a new perspective and approach to the issues and weaknesses so you can activate the strategies you learned to move toward success.

There are national music conferences held annually including the National Convention of Gospel Choirs and Choruses founded by Dr. Thomas A. Dorsey, Gospel Music Workshop of America founded by Rev. James Cleveland and the Edwin Hawkins Music and Arts. If you are unable to attend these national conferences, investigate regional and large local church conferences and workshops. These events may be easier and more economical to attend and can provide tools, skills and resources to enhance your worship arts ministry.

Plan today to attend a conference within the next 6 months or the upcoming year.

Retreat and Re-charge

Jesus then left them and went away. Matthew 16:4 (NIV)

There are times when you need to get away from everything. No singing, no performing, no learning new music, no new dances, no media meetings or anything. At times, your choir, praise team, dancers or the entire worship arts ministry together needs to take time out and get to know each other by having fun. Most of the time when a worship arts ministry is coming together it is to get ready for a performance, perfect something for a performance or be assigned a new performance task. With time so limited, there is not allotted time to get to know people so you can understand these same people so you can work together better. Food always makes people loosen up. Get people around a large pan of fried chicken, a few sides and some great desserts, let the fun begin.

Games, team building activities and small group discussions should always be a part of a retreat. Split up the groups into teams and compete for prizes.

The goal at the fun retreat does not have to be anything about worship arts just a time to enjoy each other's company and getting to know each other. In the bible, there were times that Jesus was not busy healing anybody or teaching but, just enjoying the company of his disciples and followers. Working retreats are a good time to plan the upcoming year's calendar, special music for major holidays but, try to plan one retreat, picnic or outing that is just for fun.

Re-group

But the plans of the LORD stand firm forever, the purposes of his heart through all generations. Psalm 33:11 (NIV)

Once the conferences and retreats are attended there should be some new plans made, action plans implemented and results seen from the plans implemented. The old saying goes if you fail to plan, you plan to fail. But, I add that if you don't implement your plan, you will never succeed with it. As the leader, sit down, review and pray over the information, music and resources you have received. What has God prompted you to implement? What could be implemented in the short term, i.e. 3-6 months? What could be implemented in the long term, i.e. 9 months to 1 year?

Next, sit down with your elected officers, leadership team, department heads and section leaders to brain storm, organize and draft the vision for the next level plans. If approval is necessary, get the approval from the pastor, leaders, etc. Once approval is received, roll it out to the members and do it. Don't talk about it, argue about it but just do it. There is nothing worse than receiving ideas, information and instruction but, not doing anything with it. Pray, plan, implement, re-group and watch God reward your effort.

www.ingramcontent.com/pod-product-compliance
Lightning Source LLC
Chambersburg PA
CBHW031206090426
42736CB00009B/802